STEEPLE BUSH

STEEPLE BUSH

BY

ROBERT FROST

NEW YORK

HENRY HOLT AND COMPANY

Published, May, 1947
Second Printing, June, 1947

FOR

PRESCOTT · JOHN · ELINOR · LESLEY LEE

ROBIN AND HAROLD

ORDER OF CONTENTS

A Young Birch   PAGE 3

Something for Hope   4

One Step Backward Taken   6

Directive   7

Too Anxious for Rivers   10

An Unstamped Letter in Our Rural
    Letter Box   11

To an Ancient   13

FIVE NOCTURNES

I.   *The Night Light*   17

II. *Were I in Trouble*   18

III. *Bravado*   19

IV. *On Making Certain Anything Has*
    Happened   20

V.   *In the Long Night*   21

A SPIRE AND BELFRY

A Mood Apart   PAGE 25

The Fear of God   26

The Fear of Man   27

A Steeple on the House   28

Innate Helium   29

The Courage to Be New   30

Iota Subscript   31

OUT AND AWAY

The Middleness of the Road   35

Astrometaphysical   36

Skeptic   37

Two Leading Lights   38

A Rogers Group   40

On Being Idolized   41

A Wish to Comply   42

A Cliff Dwelling   43

It Bids Pretty Fair   PAGE 44

Beyond Words   45

A Case for Jefferson   46

Lucretius versus the Lake Poets   47

EDITORIALS

Haec Fabula Docet   51

Etherealizing   52

Why Wait for Science   53

Any Size We Please   54

An Importer   55

The Planners   56

No Holy Wars for Them   57

Bursting Rapture   58

U. S. 1946 King's X   59

The Ingenuities of Debt   60

The Broken Drought   61

To the Right Person   62

STEEPLE BUSH

A Young Birch

The birch begins to crack its outer sheath
Of baby green and show the white beneath,
As whosoever likes the young and slight
May well have noticed. Soon entirely white
To double day and cut in half the dark
It will stand forth, entirely white in bark,
And nothing but the top a leafy green —
The only native tree that dares to lean,
Relying on its beauty, to the air.
(Less brave perhaps than trusting are the fair.)
And someone reminiscent will recall
How once in cutting brush along the wall
He spared it from the number of the slain,
At first to be no bigger than a cane,
And then no bigger than a fishing pole,
But now at last so obvious a bole
The most efficient help you ever hired
Would know that it was there to be admired,
And zeal would not be thanked that cut it down
When you were sick in bed or out of town.
It was a thing of beauty and was sent
To live its life out as an ornament.

Something for Hope

At the present rate it must come to pass
And that right soon that the meadow sweet
And steeple bush not good to eat
Will have crowded out the edible grass.

Then all there is to do is wait
For maple birch and spruce to push
Through meadow sweet and steeple bush
And crowd them out at a similar rate.

No plow among these rocks would pay.
So busy yourself with other things
While the trees put on their wooden rings
And with long-sleeved branches hold their sway.

Then cut down the trees when lumber grown,
And there's your pristine earth all freed
From lovely blooming but wasteful weed
And ready again for the grass to own.

A cycle we'll say of a hundred years.
Thus foresight does it and laissez faire,
A virtue in which we all may share
Unless a government interferes.

Patience and looking away ahead,
And leaving somethings to take their course.
Hope may not nourish a cow or horse,
But spes alit agricolam 'tis said.

One Step Backward Taken

Not only sands and gravels
Were once more on their travels,
But gulping muddy gallons
Great boulders off their balance
Bumped heads together dully
And started down the gully.
Whole capes caked off in slices.
I felt my standpoint shaken
In the universal crisis.
But with one step backward taken
I saved myself from going.
A world torn loose went by me.
Then the rain stopped and the blowing
And the sun came out to dry me.

Directive

Back out of all this now too much for us,
Back in a time made simple by the loss
Of detail, burned, dissolved, and broken off
Like graveyard marble sculpture in the weather,
There is a house that is no more a house
Upon a farm that is no more a farm
And in a town that is no more a town.
The road there, if you'll let a guide direct you
Who only has at heart your getting lost,
May seem as if it should have been a quarry —
Great monolithic knees the former town
Long since gave up pretence of keeping covered.
And there's a story in a book about it:
Besides the wear of iron wagon wheels
The ledges show lines ruled southeast northwest,
The chisel work of an enormous Glacier
That braced his feet against the Arctic Pole.
You must not mind a certain coolness from him
Still said to haunt this side of Panther Mountain.
Nor need you mind the serial ordeal
Of being watched from forty cellar holes
As if by eye pairs out of forty firkins.
As for the woods' excitement over you
That sends light rustle rushes to their leaves,
Charge that to upstart inexperience.
Where were they all not twenty years ago?

They think too much of having shaded out
A few old pecker-fretted apple trees.
Make yourself up a cheering song of how
Someone's road home from work this once was,
Who may be just ahead of you on foot
Or creaking with a buggy load of grain.
The height of the adventure is the height
Of country where two village cultures faded
Into each other. Both of them are lost.
And if you're lost enough to find yourself
By now, pull in your ladder road behind you
And put a sign up CLOSED to all but me.
Then make yourself at home. The only field
Now left's no bigger than a harness gall.
First there's the children's house of make believe,
Some shattered dishes underneath a pine,
The playthings in the playhouse of the children.
Weep for what little things could make them glad.
Then for the house that is no more a house,
But only a belilaced cellar hole,
Now slowly closing like a dent in dough.
This was no playhouse but a house in earnest.
Your destination and your destiny's
A brook that was the water of the house,
Cold as a spring as yet so near its source,
Too lofty and original to rage.
(We know the valley streams that when aroused
Will leave their tatters hung on barb and thorn.)

I have kept hidden in the instep arch
Of an old cedar at the waterside
A broken drinking goblet like the Grail
Under a spell so the wrong ones can't find it,
So can't get saved, as Saint Mark says they musn't.
(I stole the goblet from the children's playhouse.)
Here are your waters and your watering place.
Drink and be whole again beyond confusion.

Too Anxious for Rivers

Look down the long valley and there stands a mountain
That someone has said is the end of the world.
Then what of this river that having arisen
Must find where to pour itself into and empty?
I never saw so much swift water run cloudless.
Oh I have been often too anxious for rivers
To leave it to them to get out of their valleys.
The truth is the river flows into the canyon
Of Ceasing to Question What Doesn't Concern Us,
As sooner or later we have to cease somewhere.
No place to get lost like too far in the distance.
It may be a mercy the dark closes round us
So broodingly soon in every direction.
The world as we know is an elephant's howdah;
The elephant stands on the back of a turtle;
The turtle in turn on a rock in the ocean.
And how much longer a story has science
Before she must put out the light on the children
And tell them the rest of the story is dreaming?
"You children may dream it and tell it tomorrow."
Time was we were molten, time was we were vapor.
What set us on fire and what set us revolving
Lucretius the Epicurean might tell us
'Twas something we knew all about to begin with
And needn't have fared into space like his master
To find 'twas the effort, the essay of love.

An Unstamped Letter in Our Rural Letter Box

Last night your watch dog barked all night
So once you rose and lit the light.
It wasn't someone at your locks.
No, in your rural letter box
I leave this note without a stamp
To tell you it was just a tramp
Who used your pasture for a camp.
There pointed like the pip of spades
The young spruce made a suite of glades
So regular that in the dark
The place was like a city park.
There I elected to demur
Beneath a low-slung juniper
That like a blanket to my chin
Kept some dew out and some heat in,
Yet left me freely face to face
All night with universal space.
It may have been at two o'clock
That under me a point of rock
Developed in the grass and fern,
And as I woke afraid to turn
Or so much as uncross my feet,
Lest having wasted precious heat
I never should again be warmed,
The largest firedrop ever formed
From two stars' having coalesced

11

Went streaking molten down the west.
And then your tramp astrologer
From seeing this undoubted stir
In Heaven's firm-set firmament,
Himself had the equivalent,
Only within. Inside the brain
Two memories that long had lain,
Now quivered toward each other, lipped
Together, and together slipped;
And for a moment all was plain
That men have thought about in vain.
Please, my involuntary host,
Forgive me if I seem to boast.
'Tis possible you may have seen,
Albeit through a rusty screen,
The same sign Heaven showed your guest.
Each knows his own discernment best.
You have had your advantages.
Things must have happened to you, yes,
And have occurred to you no doubt,
If not indeed from sleeping out,
Then from the work you went about
In farming well — or pretty well.
And it is partly to compel
Myself, in forma pauperis,
To say as much I write you this.

To an Ancient

Your claims to immortality were two.
The one you made, the other one you grew.
Sorry to have no name for you but You.

We never knew exactly where to look,
But found one in the delta of a brook,
One in a cavern where you used to cook.

Coming on such an ancient human trace
Seems as expressive of the human race
As meeting someone living face to face.

We date you by your depth in silt and dust
Your probable brute nature is discussed.
At which point we are totally nonplussed.

You made the eolith, you grew the bone,
The second more peculiarly your own,
And likely to have been enough alone.

You make me ask if I would go to time
Would I gain anything by using rhyme?
Or aren't the bones enough I live to lime?

FIVE NOCTURNES

I. *The Night Light*

She always had to burn a light
Beside her attic bed at night.
It gave bad dreams and broken sleep,
But helped the Lord her soul to keep.
Good gloom on her was thrown away.
It is on me by night or day,
Who have, as I suppose, ahead
The darkest of it still to dread.

11. *Were I in Trouble*

Where I could think of no thoroughfare,
Away on the mountain up far too high,
A blinding headlight shifted glare
And began to bounce down a granite stair
Like a star fresh fallen out of the sky.
And I away in my opposite wood
Am touched by that unintimate light
And made feel less alone than I rightly should,
For traveler there could do me no good
Were I in trouble with night tonight.

III. *Bravado*

Have I not walked without an upward look
Of caution under stars that very well
Might not have missed me when they shot and fell?
It was a risk I had to take — and took.

IV. *On Making Certain Anything Has Happened*

I could be worse employed
Than as watcher of the void
Whose part should be to tell
What star if any fell.

Suppose some seed-pearl sun
Should be the only one;
Yet still I must report
Some cluster one star short.

I should justly hesitate
To frighten church or state
By announcing a star down
From say the Cross or Crown.

To make sure what star I missed
I should have to check on my list
Every star in sight.
It might take me all night.

v. *In the Long Night*

I would build my house of crystal
With a solitary friend
Where the cold cracks like a pistol
And the needle stands on end.

We would pour oil on the ingle
And for want of books recite.
We would crawl out filing single
To observe the Northern Light.

If Etookashoo and Couldlooktoo
The Esquimaux should call,
There would be fish raw and cooked too
And enough drink oil for all.

As one rankly warm insider
To another I would say,
We can rest assured on eider
There will come another day.

A SPIRE AND BELFRY

A Mood Apart

Once down on my knees to growing plants
I prodded the earth with a lazy tool
In time with a medley of sotto chants;
But becoming aware of some boys from school
Who had stopped outside the fence to spy,
I stopped my song and almost heart,
For any eye is an evil eye
That looks in on to a mood apart.

The Fear of God

If you should rise from Nowhere up to Somewhere,
From being No one up to being Someone,
Be sure to keep repeating to yourself
You owe it to an arbitrary god
Whose mercy to you rather than to others
Won't bear too critical examination.
Stay unassuming. If for lack of license
To wear the uniform of who you are,
You should be tempted to make up for it
In a subordinating look or tone
Beware of coming too much to the surface,
And using for apparel what was meant
To be the curtain of the inmost soul.

The Fear of Man

As a girl no one gallantly attends
Sets forth for home at midnight from a friend's —
She tries to make it in one catch of breath,
And this is not because she thinks of death.
The city seems intoppling from a height,
But she can trust it not to fall tonight.
(It will be taken down before it falls.)
There scarcely is a light in all its walls
Except beside a safe inside a bank
(For which assurance Mammon is to thank).
But there are little street lights she should trust
So jewel steady in the wind and dust.
Her fear is being spoken by the rude
And having her exposure misconstrued.
May I in my brief bolt across the scene
Not be misunderstood in what I mean.

A Steeple on the House

What if it should turn out eternity
Was but the steeple on our house of life
That made our house of life a house of worship?
We do not go up there to sleep at night.
We do not go up there to live by day.
Nor need we ever go up there to live.
A spire and belfry coming on the roof
Means that a soul is coming on the flesh.

Innate Helium

Religious faith is a most filling vapor.
It swirls occluded in us under tight
Compression to uplift us out of weight —
As in those buoyant bird bones thin as paper,
To give them still more buoyancy in flight.
Some gas like helium must be innate.

The Courage to Be New

I hear the world reciting
The mistakes of ancient men,
The brutality and fighting
They will never have again.

Heartbroken and disabled
In body and in mind
They renew talk of the fabled
Federation of Mankind.

But they're blessed with the acumen
To suspect the human trait
Was not the *basest* human
That made them militate.

They will tell you more as soon as
You tell them what to do
With their ever breaking newness
And their courage to be new.

Iota Subscript

Seek not in me the big I capital,
Nor yet the little dotted in me seek.
If I have in me any I at all,
'Tis the iota subscript of the Greek.

So small am I as an attention beggar.
The letter you will find me subscript to
Is neither alpha eta nor omega,
But upsilon which is the Greek for you.

OUT AND AWAY

The Middleness of the Road

The road at the top of the rise
Seems to come to an end
And take off into the skies.
So at the distant bend

It seems to go into a wood,
The place of standing still
As long the trees have stood.
But say what Fancy will,

The mineral drops that explode
To drive my ton of car
Are limited to the road.
They deal with near and far,

But have almost nothing to do
With the absolute flight and rest
The universal blue
And local green suggest.

Astrometaphysical

Lord, I have loved your sky,
Be it said against or for me,
Have loved it clear and high,
Or low and stormy;

Till I have reeled and stumbled
From looking up too much,
And fallen and been humbled
To wear a crutch.

My love for every Heaven
O'er which you, Lord, have lorded,
From number One to Seven
Should be rewarded.

It may not give me hope
That when I am translated
My scalp will in the cope
Be constellated.

But if that seems to tend
To my undue renown,
At least it ought to send
Me up, not down.

Skeptic

Far star that tickles for me my sensitive plate
And fries a couple of ebon atoms white,
I don't believe I believe a thing you state.
I put no faith in the seeming facts of light.

I don't believe I believe you're the last in space,
I don't believe you're anywhere near the last,
I don't believe what makes you red in the face
Is after explosion going away so fast.

The universe may or may not be very immense.
As a matter of fact there are times when I am apt
To feel it close in tight against my sense
Like a caul in which I was born and still am wrapped.

Two Leading Lights

I never happened to contrast
The two in the celestial cast
Whose prominence has been so vast.
The Sun is satisfied with days.
He never has in any phase
That I have heard of shone at night.
And yet he is a power of light
And could in one burst overwhelm
And dayify the darkest realm
By right of eminent domain.
He has the greatness to refrain.
The Moon for all her light and grace
Has never learned to know her place.
The notedest astronomers
Have set the dark aside for hers.
But there are many nights though clear
She doesn't bother to appear.
Some lunatic or lunar whim
Will bring her out diminished dim
To set herself beside the Sun
As Sheba came to Solomon.
It may be charitably guessed
Comparison is not her quest.
Some rumor of his wishing ring

That changes winter into spring
Has brought her merely visiting,
An irresponsible divinity
Presuming on her femininity.

A Rogers Group

How young and unassuming
They waited in the street,
With babies in their arms
And baggage at their feet.

A trolley car they hailed
Went by with clanging gong
Before they guessed the corner
They waited on was wrong.

And no one told them so
By way of traveler's aid,
No one was so far touched
By the Rogers Group they made.

On Being Idolized

The wave sucks back and with the last of water
It wraps a wisp of seaweed round my legs,
And with the swift rush of its sandy dregs
So undermines my barefoot stand I totter
And did I not take steps would be tipped over
Like the ideal of some mistaken lover.

A Wish to Comply

Did I see it go by,
That Millikan mote?
Well, I said that I did.
I made a good try.
But I'm no one to quote.
If I have a defect
It's a wish to comply
And see as I'm bid.
I rather suspect
All I saw was the lid
Going over my eye.
I honestly think
All I saw was a wink.

A Cliff Dwelling

There sandy seems the golden sky
And golden seems the sandy plain.
No habitation meets the eye
Unless in the horizon rim,
Some halfway up the limestone wall,
That spot of black is not a stain
Or shadow, but a cavern hole,
Where someone used to climb and crawl
To rest from his besetting fears.
I see the callus on his sole
The disappearing last of him
And of his race starvation slim,
Oh years ago — ten thousand years.

It Bids Pretty Fair

The play seems out for an almost infinite run.
Don't mind a little thing like the actors fighting.
The only thing I worry about is the sun.
We'll be all right if nothing goes wrong with the lighting.

Beyond Words

That row of icicles along the gutter
Feels like my armory of hate;
And you, you . . . you, you utter . . .
You wait!

A Case for Jefferson

Harrison loves my country too,
But wants it all made over new.
He's Freudian Viennese by night.
By day he's Marxian Muscovite.
It isn't because he's Russian Jew.
He's Puritan Yankee through and through.
He dotes on Saturday pork and beans.
But his mind is hardly out of his teens:
With him the love of country means
Blowing it all to smithereens
And having it all made over new.

Lucretius versus the Lake Poets

"Nature I loved; and next to Nature, Art"

Dean, adult education may seem silly.
What of it though? I got some willy-nilly
The other evening at your college deanery.
And grateful for it (Let's not be facetious!)
For I thought Epicurus and Lucretius
By Nature meant the Whole Goddam Machinery.
But you say that in college nomenclature
The only meaning possible for Nature
In Landor's quatrain would be Pretty Scenery.
Which makes opposing it to Art absurd
I grant you — if you're sure about the word.
God bless the Dean and make his deanship plenary.

EDITORIALS

EDITORIALS

Haec Fabula Docet

A Blindman by the name of La Fontaine,
Relying on himself and on his cane,
Came tap-tap-tapping down the village street,
The apogee of human blind conceit.
Now just ahead of him was seen to yawn
A trench where water pipes were laying on.
The Blindman might have found it with his ferrule,
But someone over anxious at his peril
Not only warned him with a loud command,
But ran against him with a staying hand.
Enraged at what he could but think officious,
The Blindman missed him with a blow so vicious
He gave his own poor iliac a wrench
And plunged himself head foremost in the trench:
Where with a glee no less for being grim
The workmen all turned to and buried him.

Moral

The moral is it hardly need be shown,
All those who try to go it sole alone,
Too proud to be beholden for relief,
Are absolutely sure to come to grief.

Etherealizing

A theory if you hold it hard enough
And long enough gets rated as a creed:
Such as that flesh is something we can slough
So that the mind can be entirely freed.
Then when the arms and legs have atrophied,
And brain is all that's left of mortal stuff,
We can lie on the beach with the seaweed
And take our daily tide baths smooth and rough.
There once we lay as blobs of jellyfish
At evolution's opposite extreme.
But now as blobs of brain we'll lie and dream,
With only one vestigial creature wish:
Oh may the tide be soon enough at high
To keep our abstract verse from being dry.

Why Wait for Science

Sarcastic Science she would like to know,
In her complacent ministry of fear,
How we propose to get away from here
When she has made things so we have to go
Or be wiped out. Will she be asked to show
Us how by rocket we may hope to steer
To some star off there say a half light-year
Through temperature of absolute zeró?
Why wait for Science to supply the how
When any amateur can tell it now?
The way to go away should be the same
As fifty million years ago we came —
If anyone remembers how that was.
I have a theory, but it hardly does.

Any Size We Please

No one was looking at his lonely case,
So like a half-mad outpost sentinel,
Indulging an absurd dramatic spell,
Albeit not without some shame of face,
He stretched his arms out to the dark of space
And held them absolutely parallel
In infinite appeal. Then saying, "Hell"
He drew them in for warmth of self-embrace.
He thought if he could have his space all curved
Wrapped in around itself and self-befriended,
His science needn't get him so unnerved.
He had been too all out, too much extended.
He slapped his breast to verify his purse
And hugged himself for all his universe.

An Importer

Mrs. Someone's been to Asia.
What she brought back would amaze ye.
Bamboos, ivories, jades, and lacquers,
Devil-scaring firecrackers,
Recipes for tea with butter,
Sacred rigmaroles to mutter,
Subterfuge for saving faces,
A developed taste in vases,
Arguments too stale to mention
'Gainst American invention;
Most of all the mass production
Destined to prove our destruction.
What are telephones, skyscrapers,
Safety razors, Sunday papers,
But the silliest evasion
Of the truths we owe an Asian?
But the best of her exhibit
Was a prayer machine from Tibet
That by brook power in the garden
Kept repeating Pardon, pardon;
And as picturesque machinery
Beat a sundial in the scenery —
The most primitive of engines
Mass producing with a vengeance.
Teach those Asians mass production?
Teach your grandmother egg suction.

The Planners

If anything should put an end to This,
I'm thinking the unborn would never miss
What they had never had of vital bliss.
No burst of nuclear phenomenon
That put an end to what was going on
Could make much difference to the dead and gone.
Only a few of those even in whose day
It happened would have very much to say.
And anyone might ask them who were *they*.
Who *would* they be? The guild of social planners
With the intention blazoned on their banners
Of getting one more chance to change our manners?
These anyway might think it was important
That human history should not be shortened.

No Holy Wars for Them

States strong enough to do good are but few.
Their number would seem limited to three.
Good is a thing that they the great can do,
But puny little states can only be.
And being good for these means standing by
To watch a war in nominal alliance,
And when it's over watch the world's supply
Get parcelled out among the winning giants.
God, have you taken cognizance of this?
And what on this is your divine position?
That nations like the Cuban and the Swiss
Can never hope to wage a Global Mission.
No Holy Wars for them. The most the small
Can ever give us is a nuisance brawl.

Bursting Rapture

I went to the physician to complain,
The time had been when anyone could turn
To farming for a simple way to earn;
But now 'twas there as elsewhere, any gain
Was made by getting science on the brain;
There was so much more every day to learn,
The discipline of farming was so stern,
It seemed as if I couldn't stand the strain.
But the physician's answer was "There, there,
What you complain of all the nations share.
Their effort is a mounting ecstasy
That when it gets too exquisite to bear
Will find relief in one burst. You shall see.
That's what a certain bomb was sent to be."

U. S. 1946 King's X

Having invented a new Holocaust,
And been the first with it to win a war,
How they make haste to cry with fingers crossed,
King's X — no fairs to use it any more!

The Ingenuities of Debt

These I assume were words so deeply meant
They cut themselves in stone for permanent
Like trouble in the brow above the eyes:
"Take Care to Sell Your Horse before He Dies
The Art of Life Is Passing Losses on."
The city saying it was Ctesiphon,
Which may a little while by war and trade
Have kept from being caught with the decayed,
Infirm, worn-out, and broken on its hands,
But judging by what little of it stands,
Not even the ingenuities of debt
Could save it from its losses being met.
Sand has been thrusting in the square of door
Across the tessellation of the floor,
And only rests, a serpent on its chin,
Content with contemplating, taking in,
Till it can muster breath inside a hall
To rear against the inscription on the wall.

The Broken Drought

The prophet of disaster ceased to shout.
Something was going right outside the hall.
A rain though stingy had begun to fall
That rather hurt his theory of the drought
And all the great convention was about.
A cheer went up that shook the mottoed wall.
He did as Shakespeare says, you may recall,
Good orators *will* do when they are out.
Yet in his heart he was unshaken sure
The drought was one no spit of rain could cure.
It was the drought of deserts. Earth would soon
Be uninhabitable as the moon.
What for that matter had it ever been?
Who advised man to come and live therein?

To the Right Person

In the one state of ours that is a shire,
There is a District Schoolhouse I admire
As much as anything for situation.
There are few institutions standing higher
This side the Rockies in my estimation —
Two thousand feet above the ocean level.
It has two entries for coeducation.
But there's a tight shut look to either door
And to the windows of its fenestration,
As if to say mere learning was the devil
And this school wasn't keeping any more
Unless for penitents who took their seat
Upon its doorsteps as at mercy's feet
To make up for a lack of meditation.

Notes

PAGE 4   "their wooden rings." Ripton rings.

PAGE 21   Etookashoo and Couldlooktoo who accompanied Dr. Cook to the North Pole.

PAGE 26   The Fear of God — Acknowledgment to the Papyrus Prisse

PAGE 30   The Courage to Be New

No one cavils at their killing
And being killed for speed.
Then why be so unwilling
They should do as much for creed?

PAGE 51   Haec Fabula Docet — Alternatively

The Moral is it hardly need be shown
All those who try to go it sole alone,
Or with the independence of Vermont
Are absolutely sure to come to want.

PAGE 59   U S 1946 King's X — Recent Riptonian

PAGE 60   The Ingenuities of Debt — PreFranconian